Albert Einstein

History Maker Bios

Stephanie Sammartino McPherson

BARNES & NOBLE

NEW YORK

Once again, for Jennifer, Marianne, Joseph, and Jonathan

Special thanks to my supportive editor Vicki Liestman,
whose enthusiasm for Einstein first roused my own interest.
Thanks also to Marianne Mcpherson, Angelo Sammartino,
and Richard Mcpherson for reading this manuscript
and providing their unfailing encouragement.

Illustrations by Tim Parlin

2006 Barnes & Noble Publishing

ISBN-13: 978-0-7607-3908-2
ISBN-10: 0-7607-3908-0

Printed and bound in China

5   7   9   10   8   6

TABLE OF CONTENTS

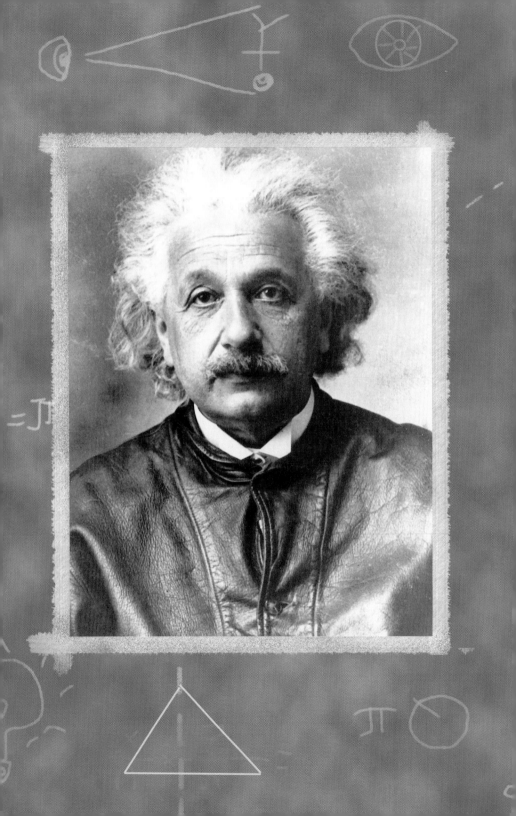

INTRODUCTION

Albert Einstein was one of the smartest scientists who ever lived. But some of Albert's questions didn't sound hard at all. What is light? What is space? What is time? Most people believed they knew all they needed to know about light and space and time. But Albert discovered that the universe is a much stranger place than anyone ever imagined.

People were amazed by Albert's ideas and fascinated by Albert. The absentminded scientist with the wild hair became known all over the world. Albert Einstein used his fame to help others and to work for world peace.

This is his story.

1 STUBBORN STUDENT

Albert Einstein wasn't the kind of boy other children noticed. For one thing, he was very quiet. For another, he didn't like sports. What Albert loved to do was think and read. School should have been lots of fun for a boy like Albert. But it wasn't.

Born March 14, 1879, Albert grew up in Munich, Germany, at a time when teachers were very strict. Students had to sit still, stay quiet, and memorize long lists of facts. They were not supposed to question what they learned.

But questioning was one of the things Albert did best. Why was there a north pole? What made magnets work? The world was full of wonders that he longed to understand.

Albert at age five

Albert's teachers didn't care about his curiosity as long as he could parrot back his lessons. That wasn't easy for him. Classmates teased Albert and called him "Honest John" because he spoke so slowly and carefully.

Math was Albert's favorite subject because there were no answers to memorize. He liked finding his own solutions. But he sometimes made mistakes adding or subtracting. His teachers did not think he was outstanding in any way.

One of the things Albert was curious about was why the needle on a compass always points north.

A Musical Family

The Einsteins were a musical family. In the evenings, Albert's mother would often play the piano while his father sang. When Albert was about six, he began taking violin lessons. At first, he didn't like them at all. He even threw a chair at his teacher. But Albert's mother made sure he kept practicing. Albert learned to love the violin and played it all of his life.

Albert's parents, Hermann and Pauline, disagreed. The Einsteins were a close, hardworking Jewish family. Together with Albert's Uncle Jakob and younger sister, Maja, Hermann and Pauline gave Albert all the attention he didn't get at school.

Uncle Jakob saw that Albert loved numbers. He began teaching his nephew some very hard math. But Albert didn't know it was supposed to be hard. He still thought solving problems was fun.

Albert was close to his sister, Maja, who was two years younger than he was.

Albert had a friend who also liked math. Max Talmud was a medical student who had dinner with the Einsteins every week. When Max gave Albert a math book as a present, Albert quickly worked through all the problems. Then he got himself even harder books. Soon twenty-two-year-old Max couldn't understand what twelve-year-old Albert was doing!

When Albert was fifteen, the Einsteins moved to Italy to start a new company. Albert was left behind to finish school.

Without his family, Albert was lonely and more bored with school than ever. His teachers still didn't understand him. When Albert asked questions, they thought he was trying to make trouble. But Albert didn't care what his teachers thought. The more uncomfortable they became, the better he liked it. Finally, Albert became so rude that his teachers expelled him. Shocked but happy to be free, he set off to join his family.

Albert was so quiet when he was young that his mother, Pauline, thought there might be something wrong with him.

Albert's father, Hermann, ran an electrical business with his brother, Jakob.

Albert felt right at home in Italy. He liked meeting people, visiting museums, and taking long hikes. At night, he gazed up at the stars.

So many ideas came to Albert when he thought about starlight and space that he just had to share them. He wrote an essay about his thoughts and sent it to his uncle Cäsar. None of Albert's teachers would have cared about Albert's ideas, but Uncle Cäsar was excited and proud.

While Albert thought about the universe, his father was thinking it was time his son finished school. Although he hadn't graduated from high school, sixteen-year-old Albert thought he could go straight to college. He shouldn't have been surprised when he failed his entrance exams. Albert was so confident, he hadn't even bothered to study. He had to finish high school after all.

2 TIME TO THINK

Albert loved his new high school. To his delight, the teachers were friendly and welcomed his questions. After graduation, he was accepted into the Polytechnic School, a famous science college in Zurich, Switzerland. He had decided to become a science teacher.

Albert was eager to learn everything he could about physics. Physics is the science of energy and matter. Matter is what everything in the universe is made of, from a planet to a toy truck.

But Albert's excitement didn't last long. He thought his teachers weren't smart enough. They didn't teach the newest, most exciting findings about the universe. Albert was still stubborn. He wouldn't do work that bored him. Often he skipped class to study on his own or to go sailing.

When he was in high school in Switzerland, Albert loved hiking through the Alps with his classmates.

At nineteen, Albert still had trouble getting along with his teachers.

Albert especially liked to talk about science with Mileva Maric, the only woman in his class. Soon she and Albert fell in love.

Mileva and Albert's other friends thought he was brilliant. Unfortunately, his professors didn't. After Albert graduated in 1900, they refused to help him find work as a college teacher. They were tired of his disrespectful ways.

Suddenly, Albert was on his own. More than anything, he wanted to marry Mileva. But first he had to find a job.

Almost two years passed before Albert found a permanent job. He wasn't a science teacher, but he enjoyed working for the Swiss Patent Office in Bern. His job was to study the plans for inventions that people sent to the office. Then he had to figure out if the inventions would work. From mousetraps to cameras, all sorts of interesting things crossed his desk.

In January 1903, Albert and Mileva were married. A year later, the couple had a little boy named Hans Albert.

RIDING A BEAM OF LIGHT

Albert loved to think about light. Sometimes he imagined what it would be like to hitch a ride on a beam of light. What would he see? He once said that he wanted to spend the rest of his life trying to figure out what light really was.

Albert with Mileva and Hans Albert. Albert loved his family, but his mind was usually on science.

Albert was still bursting with new ideas about the universe. Science made him happy in a way that nothing else did. Numbers and equations were as beautiful as poetry to him.

Luckily, Albert's job left him plenty of thinking time. When his boss disappeared from sight, Albert often grabbed a few moments to write down his thoughts. Even when he pushed Hans Albert's carriage, he kept a tablet and pencil tucked under the baby blanket just in case he needed them.

Albert was still fascinated by light. Some scientists believed a beam of light was made of billions of tiny glowing particles. Others believed that light was a wave, something like the ripples on a pond. Which group was right? Albert said they both were. He used math to prove that light is both a particle and a wave.

Albert knew that light held the key to another important discovery. He just couldn't figure out what it was. He was ready to give up when, suddenly, things that had confused him began to make sense. Eagerly, he started to write them down.

Twenty-six-year-old Albert at his desk at the Swiss Patent Office

Albert knew there was much more to light than could be seen.

Albert began with the speed of light. Nothing can make a beam of light speed up or slow down, Albert declared. Light always travels at the same rate. But time and space are different. Albert said that our measurements for time and space do change. They depend on how fast we are moving and how fast the object we want to measure is moving.

These ideas about space and time became known as the special theory of relativity. Albert just couldn't stop thinking about what it all meant. One of the things he realized was that matter can be turned into energy and energy can be turned into matter. It was an amazing thought.

If you find Albert's ideas confusing, so did the people who read the scientific papers he published. Slowly, scientists began to talk about Albert's papers. They realized how important his ideas were. They also saw that Albert was hardworking, smart, and original. This helped him get the job he had wanted all along. Finally, in 1909, Albert Einstein became a science professor.

3 WAITING FOR AN ECLIPSE

Albert's students at the University of Zurich may have noticed that his clothes were always messy and worn. Sometimes his pants were too short. And the notes for his lectures were scribbled onto tiny bits of scratch paper. But they thought he was wonderful.

Albert was never too busy to talk with students. He taught them to think for themselves and to ask questions. In fact, Albert was the kind of teacher he had always wanted himself.

In 1910, Mileva had a second son, named Eduard. Albert called his two boys "the little bears." He made toys for six-year-old Hans Albert and shared his love of music with him. Albert played his violin often.

Playing the violin helped Albert to relax and come up with new ideas.

Mileva with Eduard (LEFT) and Hans Albert (RIGHT)

Soon Albert had new job offers. He taught in the city of Prague in Austria-Hungary. Then he returned to teach at the Polytechnic School. In 1913, thirty-four-year-old Albert was asked to come to the University of Berlin in Germany. Mileva didn't want to move. But Albert put his work first. He agreed to go to Germany.

Mileva and the boys spent little time in Berlin. Almost immediately, they went back to Switzerland for a visit. Then World War I broke out in 1914.

Germany was fighting France, Britain, and many other countries in Europe. Later, the United States joined the war against Germany, too. It wasn't safe for Mileva and the children to return to Berlin.

Albert thought peace was more important than differences between nations. Instead of helping the war effort like most scientists, he lost himself in his work.

He was trying to solve the mystery of gravity. Gravity is the force that pulls things to the earth. When a ball is thrown in the air, gravity is what makes it come down.

ALBERT AND WAR

Even when he was a child, Albert had hated war. He'd refused to play soldiers like the other boys. During World War I, he helped to write a statement urging people on both sides to work for peace. Although he had been born in Germany, Albert hoped the country would lose the war.

This German poster from World War I says, "Safeguard, defend yourselves, wake up. Report to the Bavarian Army."

According to Albert, gravity didn't just pull on objects. It also pulled on light. This was part of an idea he called the general theory of relativity.

The sun has much more gravity than the earth. If Albert was right, the sun's gravity should pull on light from distant stars and make it bend. This was a very strange idea. But we can't see the light from the stars when the sun is shining. So scientists couldn't test Albert's idea.

Albert was so interested in his ideas that he neglected almost everything else. Sometimes he even forgot to eat and sleep. Finally, he wore himself out. Albert became very sick and had to stay in bed for weeks. His cousin Elsa Lowenthal, who lived in Berlin, nursed him and cooked his meals. Albert was grateful for Elsa's care and enjoyed her company.

Germany lost the war in 1918. But Mileva and the boys did not return to Berlin. In 1919, Mileva and Albert were divorced. Several months later, Albert married Elsa.

When Albert married Elsa, he also adopted her two adult daughters. He made this silhouette of his new family.

Something else important happened in 1919. There was a solar eclipse in May. During a solar eclipse, the moon passes in front of the sun and blocks its rays. Even in the middle of the day, it becomes very dark, and the stars come out.

The eclipse gave scientists a chance to test Albert's strange idea. They would be able to see if the gravity from the sun made starlight bend as it passed by.

During the eclipse, scientists took pictures of the stars and studied them closely. One of Albert's scientist friends stayed up all night, hoping to hear about their findings. But Albert went to bed as usual. He wasn't worried. He knew he was right.

4 FAMOUS OVERNIGHT

On November 6, 1919, the findings of the scientists were announced in London. Albert's theory was correct! Starlight had been bent by the sun.

The news spread quickly. Soon forty-year-old Albert faced a long line of reporters eager to talk and snap his picture.

Albert getting his picture taken. He was never very comfortable with being famous.

The sudden fuss took Albert by surprise. He didn't want to be famous. He had no time for it! But Albert knew what really mattered. He decided to make reporters pay to take his picture. The money went to feed hungry children still suffering from the war.

People were fascinated by Albert's ideas. They also enjoyed his humor and honesty. The public couldn't hear enough about the brilliant scientist with the warm eyes and laughter that could fill a room. Some people even named their babies after Albert.

Not everyone loved Albert, however. Many Germans were still angry about losing the war and unfairly blamed Jews. Since Albert was Jewish, they criticized him and his work.

It had become hard for Jewish students to get accepted at universities and for Jewish professors to get jobs. In 1921, Albert agreed to go to the United States to help raise money to create a university in Jerusalem, a city in Palestine. It was to be a center of learning where Jews from all over the world would be welcome.

Albert and Elsa arriving in the United States in 1921

Albert didn't really care if his clothes were messy. He had more important things to think about.

When Albert and Elsa's ship docked in New York, reporters rushed to meet them. The same thing happened all over the country. Albert still preferred his privacy. But he believed his appearances helped lessen the anger that some Americans still felt toward Germany after the war.

Albert went to see the battlefields in France in 1922. He was saddened by the ruined villages. He thought if everyone could see what he saw, then people would work harder to prevent war.

Later that year, Albert and Elsa were on their way to Japan when a telegram arrived on the ship. It said that Albert had won the 1921 Nobel Prize in physics for the work he had done years before showing that light was both a particle and a wave. The Nobel Prize was one of the most important awards in the world. It was a great honor.

PLAYFUL GENIUS

Albert loved jokes. Sometimes he took over the elevator in his apartment building. Playfully, he pushed the buttons so that the elevator would stop on all the wrong floors. His fellow passengers may have grumbled, but his family accepted his funny quirks. They liked to tease Albert by calling him "the genius." This always made him laugh.

Through the years, Albert and Elsa made
several more trips to the United States.
They were in Pasadena, California, early in
1933 when they learned that Adolf Hitler
had been made one of the leaders of
Germany. Hitler was a man who hated
Jews and would do anything for power.
The people who supported him were called
Nazis.

Later that year, Albert and Elsa learned
that Nazi soldiers had broken into their
apartment in Berlin. Horrified and angry,
they realized that it was too dangerous for
them to return to Germany.

5 AMERICAN SCIENTIST

After spending the summer of 1933 in Belgium, Albert and Elsa returned to the United States and settled in Princeton, New Jersey. They bought a house in a quiet neighborhood that was close to Albert's new job at the Institute for Advanced Study.

Albert's house in Princeton, New Jersey, at 112 Mercer Street

Soon the townsfolk got used to seeing Albert walk to and from his office. His clothes were baggy. His hair was so wild that one child said he looked like a lion. Strangest of all, Albert didn't wear socks, not even when he went to visit President Franklin D. Roosevelt. He thought that socks were too much trouble to mend.

But it was never too much trouble to talk to the children he met or stop to admire a new baby. He always found time to enjoy a good laugh or help someone in need. He taught one neighborhood child to ride a bike. And once, he played his violin for some children who came trick-or-treating.

When Elsa became seriously ill, Albert began working at home so he could be constantly near her. In December 1936, Elsa died. More than ever, Albert needed work to keep his mind off his great sadness.

When Albert went to work at the Institute for Advanced Study, he asked for a big trash can so he could throw away all of his mistakes.

For years, Albert had been trying to figure out how all the forces of nature fit together. It was to be a great theory of everything. He called it the unified field theory. Many scientists did not believe it could be done. But Albert was as stubborn as he'd always been. If he believed something, he would keep on trying to prove it.

Albert still hated the very idea of war. But Germany continued to harm Jews and to be a danger to Europe. That was why Albert signed a letter to President Roosevelt urging the United States to develop an atomic bomb before the Germans did.

ALBERT EINSTEIN, AMERICAN

Albert liked the freedom and welcome he found in the United States. On October 1, 1940, reporters gathered to watch him become a United States citizen. One month later, Albert voted in his first election. He cast his vote for President Franklin D. Roosevelt.

Hitler's soldiers march into Austria after taking over the country in 1938.

An atomic bomb was a weapon with so much power, it was terrible to think about. Some of Albert's own work had made it possible. Albert hoped with all his heart it would never be used. But he knew that if Germany got the bomb first, the entire world would be in danger.

In September 1939, Germany invaded Poland and World War II began. Deeply worried, Albert sent two more letters to the president.

The United States entered the war in 1941 when Japan attacked Hawaii. There was fighting all over the world. In 1945, terrible news came from Germany. Hitler had murdered six million Jews. Albert was heartsick and furious.

On August 6, 1945, Albert was coming downstairs after a nap when he heard more terrible news. The United States had dropped an atomic bomb on Japan.

The U.S. dropped a second atomic bomb on Japan on August 9, 1945, and ended the war.

Albert's office at the Institute for Advanced Study

Albert was so upset he could hardly speak. For the rest of his life, Albert warned nations about the dangers of atomic weapons. He never missed a chance to promote world peace.

Albert was so admired that in 1952, he was asked to become the president of the new Jewish nation of Israel. Albert would do almost anything for the Jewish people. But he had to turn down the presidency. At age seventy-three, he said he was too old and that his work kept him too busy.

Albert didn't take himself very seriously. But other people did. In 1999, TIME magazine named him the "Person of the Century."

Albert never stopped working. He kept trying to find a unified field theory. When he was rushed to the hospital shortly after his seventy-sixth birthday, he asked someone to bring him his glasses, paper, and a pencil. He wanted to spend his last days doing what he loved best. He died on April 18, 1955.

People are still fascinated by Albert Einstein. He has been honored over and over again. His face is on postage stamps, and a crater on the moon is named after him. Albert once said, "I am neither especially clever nor especially gifted. I am only very, very curious." Thanks to Albert's curiosity, our view of the universe will never be the same.

TIMELINE

ALBERT EINSTEIN
WAS BORN ON
MARCH 14, 1879.

In the year . . .

1895   Albert was expelled from school.

1900   he graduated from the Polytechnic School, a   Age 21
college in Switzerland.

1902   he joined the Swiss Patent Office.

1903   he married Mileva Maric.   Age 23

1904   his son Hans Albert was born.

1905   he published the special theory of relativity.   Age 26

1910   his son Eduard was born.

1916   he published the general theory of   Age 37
relativity.

1919   he and Mileva were divorced.
an eclipse proved his general theory of   Age 40
relativity.
he married his cousin Elsa Lowenthal.

1921   he traveled to the United States to raise
money for the Hebrew University.

1922   he won the 1921 Nobel Prize in physics.   Age 43

1933   he joined the Institute for Advanced
Study in Princeton, New Jersey.

1936   Elsa died.   Age 57

1940   he became an American citizen.

1952   he turned down the chance to become
president of Israel.

1955   he died on April 18.   Age 76

CAN YOU THINK LIKE EINSTEIN?

You might have heard of Einstein's famous equation $E=mc^2$. But do you know what it means? It's really just a multiplication problem. You can also write the equation like this: $E = m \times c \times c$. (The number 2 next to the letter c means that you should multiply c times itself.) The letter E stands for energy. The letter m stands for mass. Mass is a measurement of how much material is in an object. Finally, the letter c in the equation stands for the speed that light travels through space. This is a very big number—about 186,000 miles per second.

So what does $E=mc^2$ mean? It is an equation that tells us how much energy we can get out of a certain object. Just multiply the object's mass by the speed of light twice, and you've got the energy. Even if the mass is very small, it can be turned into a huge amount of energy because light travels so fast. If this makes sense to you, you're thinking like Einstein!

FURTHER READING

NONFICTION
Gold-Dworkin, Heidi. *Exploring Light and Color.* **New York: McGraw-Hill, 1999.** An introduction to the science of light and color. Includes experiments.

FICTION
Harness, Cheryl. *Ghosts of the Twentieth Century.* **New York: Simon & Schuster, 2000.** Albert Einstein takes a young boy visiting a museum on a tour of the twentieth century.

Kerr, Judith. *When Hitler Stole Pink Rabbit.* **New York: Putnam, 1999.** A nine-year-old Jewish girl and her family flee from Germany when Hitler comes to power.

Wishinsky, Frieda. *What's the Matter with Albert?* **Toronto: Maple Tree Press, 2002.** A young boy interviews Albert Einstein for his school paper. He learns about Einstein's difficulties in school, his scientific achievements, and his work for peace. Illustrated with art and photographs.

WEBSITES

Einstein Archives
This website includes photographs and information about the life of Albert Einstein. It also has an "Einstein for Kids" page.

The Jewish-American Hall of Fame
<amuseum.org/jahf/> This website includes information about the life of Albert Einstein, photographs of medals and coins from around the world commemorating Einstein, and an Einstein quiz.

SELECT BIBLIOGRAPHY

Brian, Denis. *Einstein: A Life.* New York: John Wiley & Sons, Inc., 1996.

Clark, Ronald W. *Einstein: The Life and Times.* 2nd ed. New York: Avon Books, 1984.

Einstein, Albert. *The Collected Papers of Albert Einstein, Vol. I, The Early Years, 1879–1902.* Trans. Anna Beck. Princeton, New Jersey: Princeton University Press, 1987.

Einstein, Albert. *The World As I See It.* Trans. Alan Harris. New York: The Citadel Press, 1984.

Frank, Philipp. *Einstein: His Life and Times.* Ed. Shuichi Kusaka. Trans. George Rosen. New York: Da Capo Press, Inc., 1989.

Hoffmann, Banesh, with the collaboration of Helen Dukas. *Albert Einstein: Creator and Rebel.* New York: The Viking Press, 1972.

Pais, Abraham. *Einstein Lived Here.* New York: Oxford University Press, 1994.

Pais, Abraham. *'Subtle is the Lord . . . ': The Science and the Life of Albert Einstein.* New York: Oxford University Press, 1982.

Sayen, Jamie. *Einstein in America: The Scientist's Conscience in the Age of Hitler and Hiroshima.* New York: Crown Publishers, Inc., 1985.

White, Michael, and John Gribben. *Einstein: A Life in Science.* New York: Dutton, 1994.

INDEX

Acknowledgments

For photographs and artwork: Princeton University Library, p. 4; Courtesy of the Albert Einstein Archives, the Jewish National and University Library, the Hebrew University of Jerusalem, Israel, pp. 7, 10, 11, 12, 18, 19, 24, 27, 31; © Dr. John Cunningham/Visuals Unlimited, p. 8; © Van der Heyden Collection/Independent Picture Service, p. 15; Lotte Jacobi Collection, University of New Hampshire, p. 16; © Australian Picture Library/CORBIS, p. 20; © Nancy Smedstad/Independent Picture Service, p. 23; The Art Archive/Eileen Tweedy, p. 26; Ullstien Bild, p. 30; © Bettmann/CORBIS, pp. 32, 41, 42; Alan Richards/Courtesy of the Archives of the Institute for Advanced Study, p. 36; © CORBIS, p. 37; National Archives, pp. 39, 40. Front cover, Illustrated London News. Back cover, © Robert Shaw/CORBIS. **For quoted material:** p. 43, Denis Brian, *Einstein: A Life* (New York: John Wiley & Sons, Inc., 1996).